When The Trust is Broken

by Sharon Grace

Paula,
"Chloe" Thanks you!
Sharon

1

First Edition: February 2009
Printed in the United States of America
ISBN13 – 9780615270968

Author Contact Information:
Website: www.Sharongrace.com
Email: Sharongrace@rochester.rr.com

Edited by Barbara-Ann Clifton

Acknowledgements:

To my Husband:
For the unconditional love, support, and patience. For the energy, enthusiasm and inspiration you give me each day. For believing in me more than I believed in myself and encouraging the completion of this book.

To my Children:
The greatest gifts in life, and giving purpose to mine. You have been challenged to overcome adversity and rejection. I could not be more proud for who you are and what you have become. Your strength and endurance continue to inspire me.
I am proud to be your Mom.

To my additional Children:
Thank you for your love and support and the joy you have added to my life.

To my Mother:
Whose loving relationship with me has come full circle.

To Shirley and Red:
Who have stood by me during every crisis and event in my adult life.
Who taught me confidence and the gift of giving from the heart.

To my Family, Friends, and Girls Club:
You have inspired me more than you know.

To Jean:
My sister and my best friend who never once walked
away or ever let anyone or anything come between us.
Who gave my children a lifetime of love and support.

To Greg and Sue:
The best friends anyone could ask for!
Your help, support, and encouragement to keep things
in their perspective was greatly appreciated. As well as
reminding me it's OK to laugh.

To my friend Dan:
For your countless hours of support to make this book
possible.

To my friend Jean T:
Who has listened to almost every speech I have ever
written and endless material for my motivational
programs as well as my book.

To the Bivona Child Advocacy Center:
Kathie and Lou Bivona for your generosity and life's
devotion to the success of providing a safe place,
services and support for children of sexual and
physical abuse.

**To The National Center for Missing and
Exploited Children, New York Branch:**
For your help with prevention of child abduction and
sexual exploitation; finding missing children;
assisting victims of child abduction and sexual
exploitation, their families, and the professionals who
serve them.

**To The Monroe County District Attorney and
Assistant District Attorneys of The Child
Abuse and Domestic Violence Bureau:**
For the conscious effort you make and the thankless
hours of work on behalf of all of the children who are
victims of sexual and other abuses.

Most of all—My Grandchildren:
Like finding a rare and precious gem, each in a setting
of their own.
A mother's ultimate reward and compliment to her
family.
For allowing me to be your voice and teaching me the
importance of making a difference in the lives of other
children.

This book is especially dedicated to:

My little diddle dumplin'

This book is dedicated to Chloe, a child who's been robbed of her innocence by the ruthless behavior of a trusted adult and a system that failed her before she had a chance to fight back.

On a personal level, nothing satisfies me more than knowing we've had the privilege of helping children like Chloe regain confidence in themselves and learn to trust that not all older people are bad; that there are, in fact, a lot of people that fundamentally do care about their well being and happiness. And, have the strength of character to stand up for them.

Thanks to the wonderful staff of the Bivona Child Advocacy Center for their commitment and labor of love on behalf of all the children who cross our path. With your help and dedication, many kids like Chloe and their families have a better chance in life.

Chloe, may you grow up to be a brave young woman; that you fulfill your dreams and aspirations to become an accomplished member of your community; and live a happy, full life.

God bless you.

Lou Bivona

I will never forget the look on my granddaughter's face when she told me about the 'bad man' and what you did to her.

Sharon Grace to Michael Bennett,
Monroe County Court, June 13, 2007

PROLOGUE

One warm September evening, my husband John and I went to visit my daughter Morgan and her family. We were all sitting in the living room, talking casually and playing with the children, when our attention was suddenly drawn to the six o'clock news playing in the background.

"Our top story tonight focuses on allegations of sexual abuse of a four-year-old girl at a Penfield daycare center," the male announcer said.

Everyone in the room stopped what they were doing. We were stunned by the news, especially since my grandchildren had recently attended a Penfield daycare center.

Then a photo appeared on the screen of the man who'd been arrested for the crime. Aside from his orange, prison-issue jumpsuit, he looked like a pretty normal guy, someone you might see at the grocery store, the post office or church.

He was a husband, a father and someone's son. But to me, he was the monster that committed this horrific, unthinkable crime. Not once, not twice, but multiple times.

When I turned to look at my four-year-old granddaughter Chloe, I saw she was paralyzed with fear. She seemed terrified by what she had seen on TV. The expression on her face told me immediately that something was terribly wrong. Instantly, all of the signs from the past months made sense to me. Her eyes widened, her head jerked backward and her mouth opened wide. Then she covered it with her tiny hand as she gasped for a breath, pointed at the television and screamed, "Nana, that is the *bad* man. Do you know what he did to me-e-e-e-e?"

Oh—my—God!

That single moment changed our lives forever.

CHAPTER 1

The trust we place in people is something we take for granted every single day. Without trust, our society would fall apart. When we're driving down the highway at fifty-five miles per hour, we trust that the person in the oncoming car isn't going to cross the yellow line. When we're in a grocery store, we trust that the food we buy is safe to eat. We trust our doctors' decisions and that the medications they prescribe will help us heal.

We have learned many times and in many ways to trust. We teach our children to build trusting relationships with teachers, coaches, bus drivers, priests, politicians, firemen, police officers —the list goes on and on. But sometimes it's challenging to try and establish trust without promoting mistrust.

Unfortunately, some of the people we trust most wind up slipping through the cracks. And when that happens, we can't rewind the clock.

*****

Every family struggles with some type of dysfunction. I believe that no matter who you are, where you live or what you have, at some point in life, everyone is challenged by the unexpected. One thing I know for sure is that strength, attitude and faith brought this 55-year-old daughter, wife, mother and nana to it, through it and, eventually, beyond it.

I had always been the type of person who tried to put her best face forward, just like I was taught to do: hair groomed, nails polished and makeup done, even on days I didn't go to work. My clothes were always pressed and appropriate for the occasion. My shoes and bag had to match, and even my jewelry was well coordinated.

Although I seemed pretty together on the outside, I hid the pain, the hurt, the secret suffering and the growing fear of the unknown for many years. I found it difficult to trust anyone, and I found myself growing skeptical and more suspicious. But I'm getting ahead of myself.

From a very young age, it was apparent how much I loved to help other people. I've always tried to make a difference, by solving problems, consoling those in pain or just offering a soft shoulder to cry on. I especially enjoyed caring for and attending to the needs of children.

Aside from watching my younger siblings, my first real babysitting job was for the daughters of my orthodontist. It was in their big blue house at the end of a cul-de-sac where my love for children really blossomed.

Each time I entered their house, which was just about every weekend, I felt a great sense of responsibility. Not only did I have fun feeding, bathing and telling bedtime stories to those lovely blonde-haired little girls, but I gained quite a bit of experience, too. I grew my business and babysat for friends and neighbors all the way through high school. At the time, I thought fifty cents an hour—and seventy-five cents after midnight—was really good money!

As far back as I can remember I've always been interested in talking to people. Because of my social nature and my interest in personal grooming, it was only natural that I developed a penchant for hairstyling at an early age. At first I worked on my dolls' hair, and then when I was twelve I gave my first live haircut—to my younger sister on family portrait day!

While in high school, I attended beauty school and began my career as a stylist. After graduation, I meshed the two things I enjoyed doing most...talking to people and making them feel good about themselves. I thought I was off to a pretty good start, but the next two decades proved extremely challenging.

Since I grew up in a very large family, I was expected to go to high school, get a job, get married and raise a family. I did just that, all in the right order. I'm not sure if I did it to escape my family situation or because I thought it was the right thing to do. If only I knew then what I know now, maybe I would not have been as trusting or have allowed so many bad things to happen in my life.

I had really looked forward to having a family and living a happy life. I was the third of seven children and the first daughter. There was always a baby around, always a youngster in a car seat and always someone to take care of. I truly enjoyed taking responsibility for the younger children, and I especially loved getting them up first thing in the morning. They had such a look of innocence, and that sweet, fresh smell of Johnson's baby powder that they'd been sprinkled with the night before. I would parade them up and down the street in the stroller, so proud to be the big sister.

As I watched my mother hover over the little ones, gently teaching them to walk and talk, I could only hope to be as loving with my own children someday. She didn't make it look very hard. Get the children up, feed them and send them off to school. Do your chores and errands, make dinner, have coffee with neighbors or relatives, send the children to bed and start all over again the next day. I could handle that, I thought.

Like my own mother, I married at the young age of nineteen. But unlike her, my first child didn't arrive for another five years. I'd been told that my chances of bearing children were slim because of a prior medical diagnosis, which I had a difficult time accepting. I couldn't imagine not having children, especially since I felt so well prepared to care for them. What I *wasn't* prepared for was such a crushing disappointment. Imagine *me* not having children! I had dreamed of being a mother all my life. I knew there were alternatives, and I would have considered them all, especially adoption.

But then one day, after exhibiting an extraordinary amount of patience, I finally heard my doctor say the words I'd longed to hear—"You're pregnant, and everything looks good."

At that moment, I was convinced that miracles really do happen.

I couldn't believe it. I wanted to jump up and down, and tell the whole world I was having a baby! I would get to wake up every morning and go to bed each night with a child of my very own to love and nurture. I was overwhelmed by emotions, both anxious and excited about the many wonderful experiences that awaited me. I wanted so much to be a mother, and I prayed that I'd be a really good one to this child. My family would mean everything to me.

Those nine and a half months went by more quickly than I expected, and on that Thanksgiving night, I ended up with much more than just indigestion after my turkey dinner. Early the next morning, my lifelong dream was fulfilled. I delivered a beautiful, healthy baby boy and named him Michael. Every gift I received was blue, from clothes and pajamas to knitted blankets. Even the toys and building blocks came in all shades of the color.

Then, just as I was adjusting to motherhood, I was blessed with another miracle. I became pregnant again, and this time around, our house was filled with pink, pink, and more pink. I gave birth to a baby girl named Morgan.

At that point, it seemed like I had it all: a son, a daughter and a nice home. It was exactly what I'd envisioned during all those years of babysitting. Of course, alcohol abuse and inappropriate behavior weren't part of the perfect life I'd planned for myself. But they turned out to be the elements that destroyed my marriage soon after Morgan was born. Our family life was shattered before it ever really began. Had I not seen the signs or had I chose to overlook them? Having grown up in a family plagued by alcohol issues, I thought I would have known better than to put myself in such a position. I never believed I would make that kind of mistake, and the fact that I did made me feel like such a failure.

The divorce was final, but my guilt and shame lived on. There I was, a single mom with two small children and a fractured fairy tale for a life.

What would people think? What would happen to my children? I knew they were too young to feel any kind of emotional attachment to their father or understand what they would be missing in their lives. Regardless, I worried about how this life change would affect them later on.

No matter how horrible I felt about what had happened, I knew I had to move on. It didn't take long for me to realize I'd been handed a tremendous responsibility. But there was no turning back, and my children were all that mattered. Somehow I managed to learn how to balance taking care of my kids, working hard and even having a little fun when I could find the time.

For instance, my girlfriends suggested that I join a softball league. They thought I might be spending too much time on my children and not enough time on myself. As much as I loved sharing all the daily activities with Michael and Morgan, I had to admit I secretly craved adult interaction.

The decision to join the softball team proved to be a good one. I found the experience very rewarding, and I made many lasting friendships.

I brought my children to the games because leaving them home with a sitter was not an option. I felt much more comfortable having them close to me, and I didn't really trust them with too many people. Taking them to the games also provided a great opportunity for them to learn how to behave in public. And it helped me teach them how to respect others and communicate well, two life skills that had always been important to me.

I thought that having my children see me from a different perspective would help establish a bond of trust between us. And besides, they enjoyed sitting on the sidelines and rooting for their mother. Not to mention all the attention they received from the other adults.

It was through my softball league that I met my second husband, who was actually one of my coaches. He seemed like a very nice man and took an immediate interest in my children. As soon as I got to know him better, we started doing things together with the children, including picnics, parties and even outings with friends.

While we were dating, I had a serious car accident that left me with a minor brain injury. It happened during a driving rainstorm on a Rochester expressway, when a tractor-trailer ran my new-to-me Camaro off the road. I had just picked up the freshly painted car a few days before, from the father of my best friend. It took me four months to recover and a whole year to heal completely.

During my recovery period, my children spent most of their time with our sitter, whom they lovingly called Aunt Mamie. When the other moms came to pick up their children, they would ask how I was doing. Aunt Mamie told me Morgan would repeatedly say, "Do you know why my Mom didn't die in her car accident? Because she has two lovely children!" That thought has stayed with me ever since and been a driving force in my life.

Less than a year later, after being in a coma for eight days, my youngest brother died, the result of a tragic motorcycle accident. He was only nineteen years old. Crushed by sadness, I thought I had felt every emotion there was to feel...until I stood over his grave as hundreds of balloons were released in the air and the song "Free Bird" played in the background. But I kept my head held high; I didn't want to look weak. I was still too tough to cry in front of anyone. Looking back now, how I wish I had cried for my baby brother.

Around the same time, my coach was also in an automobile accident, which he miraculously survived. After so much tragedy, I was emotionally worn out.

Relying on each other for strength, the coach and I continued to develop our relationship. We bought an old farmhouse in the country and decided to get married. He also began adoption proceedings to insure that my young children would be given roots, stability and the same last name.

Our new life kept us very busy. We both had full-time jobs, and we spent many hours caring for our ninety acres of land, which we'd turned into a Christmas tree farm.

After months of remodeling our home, we woke up one cold February morning to find the family room flooded. Apparently, some of the pipes had burst during the night. We got started right away on repairing the damage, which required us to replace all the floors and walls.

As we continued to pour our blood, sweat and tears into the house, we got another big surprise. But this time the news was good, and soon we were preparing for an addition of another kind.

Chapter 2

A year and a day after our wedding, I gave birth to my second son, Blake. It had been nine years since Morgan was born, and the joy I felt far exceeded my expectations. Another miracle!

Life had certainly changed over the years and changed for the better. We were now a big, happy family, all living together in a large but cozy farmhouse. We entertained often; our family and friends would drive out to the country to enjoy a tractor ride, a walk around the property or a quiet afternoon with the kids.

Because he was so much younger than our other children, Blake was always the center of everyone's attention. Michael and Morgan would fight to have a turn at holding and feeding him. I promised both of them that they'd always have a part in caring for their little brother. Little did they know they'd get more than they bargained for!

Both Michael and Morgan helped me with baths, feedings, diaper changes and, of course, playtime. Because the four of us were always together, I found myself cherishing my time alone with Blake on the drive to work each morning. I was also lucky enough to be able to bring him to work with me because at the time I owned my own hair salon. But most days, I chose to leave him with my sister Jean, who had two toddlers of her own at home. They were all delighted to spend time with my little guy.

On school holidays, Jean would watch all three of my children if needed. A houseful of children never fazed her. I couldn't have found anyone I trusted more to watch my kids, as Jean is not only my sister but also my closest friend.

Eight months later, as our new family was just settling into the rhythms of a comfortable domestic life, tragedy struck once again.

It was New Year's Day 1988. After spending a wonderful evening with friends, toasting with champagne and watching the famous ball drop, we were awakened at four in the morning by the barking of our dog. He was a black Labrador retriever named Moose, who later made national news and gained notoriety for saving our lives. He barked uncontrollably at the flames shooting through our house, alerting us to the vicious fire that destroyed our beautifully renovated home.

The loss was cruel and devastating. The fire had burned the walls and charred the rafters, and the water and smoke damage were extensive. Many of our personal possessions were destroyed—all those material things we had worked so hard for but now didn't seem to matter.

We were just blessed that our children, and the family of three staying with us for the holiday, were all safe. When we'd realized what was happening, the adults had grabbed the children and breathlessly run across the road, going as fast as we could through a foot of snow. We pounded on the neighbors' door, yelling for help and shouting, "Fire, fire!" The neighbors, who also had overnight guests, came running out of the house, thinking that it was *their* home that was on fire.

They quickly called for help and soon the firemen arrived. As I watched them battle the flames, I didn't even feel the cold. I think I was too numb or too frozen...or maybe both. It was ironic that a few short hours ago we had been watching people celebrate in Times Square. Who would have imagined that before the sun came up we would be standing outside in below-zero temperatures, watching our house burn down?

I just wanted to wake up from this terrible nightmare.

The haunting memories of the sirens of five fire companies and the questions from the arson squad are forever etched in my mind. I remember becoming hysterical during the questioning, but I understood later that the investigators were just doing their jobs. At the time, I was angry at their questions. I thought to myself, *Who on earth would start their own house on fire, especially with their children in it?*

I was relieved when the investigators finally discovered the cause of the fire. A spark had escaped the spark arrester in the chimney and lodged itself in the roof. The fire had started down the back wall of the house, which was part of Blake's bedroom.

For the second time in as many days, my children and I had escaped a near-death situation. Just two days earlier, I'd been nearing an exit ramp on the highway when my car engine overheated and was suddenly engulfed in flames. I'd pulled over as fire and smoke billowed from my Subaru wagon. I'd jumped out of the car and grabbed Blake, still in his car seat, all the while screaming for Michael and Morgan to get out of the car.

And now, after watching my house burn down, I couldn't think of anything else that could possibly go wrong.

We were blessed, however, by the incredible outpouring of support from family, friends, neighbors and the community. We received clothes, food, furniture and boxes of incidentals, as well as baby supplies. It amazed me how many anonymous donors came forward and gave so generously to my family. How does one begin to thank an entire community?

We stayed with extended family for a while and then spent some time at a motel. We eventually rented a furnished home on a nearby lake, planning to stay until our renovations were completed. We filled plastic garbage bags with clothes and other items that had been given to us, and moved into the lake house. Before we could unpack, however, the bags were accidentally mistaken for garbage and put out to the curb. No one realized the mistake until it was too late.

I had to wonder...was some sort of black cloud floating over me?

Sharon Grace

Chapter 3

We spent our days monitoring the progress as our home was being rebuilt. We called our dog Moose "the Supervisor," since he was always outside watching everyone come and go. He had a lead attached to his collar, which gave him plenty of freedom to run between the garage and the barn.

One day while I was at work, my husband and the two older kids went outside to feed Moose. They were horrified to find that the dog had strangled himself with his lead. Even though they were devastated, they buried Moose before Blake and I got home because they knew I couldn't take any more pain.

But it ended up being too much for my poor children to bear, too. They had lost their home, their toys, their clothes...and now their beloved dog. Things were definitely not going well for my family.

But as always, we kept moving forward. I began spending a lot of time reading self-help books at the public library. I relied on my closest family and friends. And I tried not to ask for too many favors from up above.

One day a friend said to me, "God doesn't give you more than you can handle."

I said, "Thank you, God—enough already!"

As our home underwent several lengthy renovations, my husband's abuse of alcohol became alarmingly more apparent. I was beginning to fear that my marriage was falling apart. I tried so hard to understand what was happening and really make things work. I even attended Alcoholics Anonymous meetings so the children and I could learn to cope. Then I realized this problem was too big for me to fix. I was extremely angry and bitter, at my husband and myself. I worried about how this would affect my children because they had already experienced so much loss. I blamed myself for the pain I knew this would cause them. Had I really allowed this to happen again?

The stress took its toll on my body, and I became physically ill. I developed back problems that required years of physical therapy. I had three operations within one year, including a radical hysterectomy.

My children were my only source of energy and hope. They gave me a reason to go on. They were my sole purpose in life. What would I ever do without them?

I was mad at myself for having my priorities so mixed up. Why had I always tried so hard to please the men in my life? I guess I was constantly seeking male approval, ever since I was a little girl. Maybe if my father had taken more of an interest in me, it would have prevented me from making such bad decisions. But I had to stop making excuses for my own choices.

I tried to be strong, but my insecurities began to take over. My childhood memories came flooding back to me. The ridicule, the mockery, the mental cruelty I had suffered from my father, and then from my first two husbands. I remembered the unkind words, the physical abuse and the criticism that had left very deep scars. And it was all because of alcohol.

Needing to talk to someone, I turned to my family doctor. After telling him about some of my emotional pain, he told me, "Sharon, you're an enabler."

I asked, "What exactly do you mean by that?"

He said that it's in my nature to help people and make them feel good about themselves. Therefore, I tend to overlook their weaknesses and focus only on their strengths. By building them up, I indirectly encourage them to continue their destructive behaviors. He also said, "Try not to dwell on it. Your children need you now more than ever."

Don't dwell on it? How do you put something like that aside? All I wanted to do was run away, get in the car and keep driving until I reached Happytown, U.S.A. I wondered if such a place even existed. Because the place I was in...well, it could only be described as hell.

But I couldn't leave. My children didn't deserve any of this, and the doctor was right. They needed me.

I also agreed with his assessment that I'm too protective of those I love. I tried to stay positive, but I was mentally exhausted. I wasn't feeling so great physically, either. I had lost a lot of weight; I was barely one hundred pounds soaking wet.

Not only was I dealing with the structural damage caused by the fire, but I soon discovered that my house was actually making me sick. Mold and other allergens that resulted from poor workmanship while our house was being rebuilt caused me some pretty serious health issues. I had always enjoyed my work, but it came to a point where I had no choice but to close my hair salon. I was too sick to continue running my own business.

It was devastating to have to give up the salon. I had worked so hard to build my business, and I'd enjoyed thirteen wonderful years of meaningful relationships with my clients and their families. But, after fainting and having to be carried out to an ambulance hooked up to an oxygen tank, I knew it was time to close the door.

I became very depressed and did not speak to anyone for weeks.

Although it felt like my world was caving in, I forced myself to volunteer at Blake's daycare center. I was working with toddlers and preschoolers, which really helped me develop a sense of humor. They were so precious and innocent. I could never understand why anyone would ever want to hurt a child.

When I could no longer afford to pay for daycare, I became even more depressed. I was blind when it came to seeing one door open after another one had closed.

Some call it tunnel vision, but I couldn't see the forest for the trees. But one day Blake said something that turned my whole life around. He said, "Mommy, you are so sad. If you don't go back to work, I can't go to school, and I will never see my friends again."

At that point, I realized that this little child had feelings and was trying to express them. I couldn't change what had already happened in our lives, but I now knew how much I needed to change my attitude.

I started to remind myself of the values that have always defined me: trust, faith, integrity. One day I looked in the mirror and said, "Come on, get yourself together. What are you gaining here? Start hanging out with people who lift you up, not bring you down. People who see the good in you. Walk away from the rest."

That pep talk eventually did the trick. I went back to school to earn my teaching certification and became an instructor at a popular school of hair design. Even though I was teaching adults, it was very much like working with children, since practically everything I taught them was new.

It was so gratifying to help my students grow, achieve and succeed in the industry that I couldn't wait to go to work each day. My new role motivated me to connect with people, which changed my whole attitude. I began to set goals and believe in myself again. I also joined a group called Toastmasters to improve my communication skills. I attended many conferences and educational classes with people who thrived on success, all of which had a positive influence on my life.

One day I was asked to fill in for the stylist at a nursing home salon. I agreed to do the job for six weeks. But as it often happens in life, six weeks turned into ten years, and I still work there two days a week. Back then, working part time provided the flexibility I needed to be at home with my children.

Everything seemed to be going so well, but life still had a few surprises up its sleeve.

CHAPTER 4

For the second time in my life, I found myself a single mom. But this time I had three children to care for and even greater challenges to face.

Divorce brought heartache to all of us. The children faced abandonment and rejection issues, while I dealt with loneliness and guilt. Each time I divorced, it ended all communication with my former husband. My exes were totally out of the picture. It was hard for the children to keep losing their fathers like that.

To help make up for their loss, I constantly professed my love to them. I always wanted my children to feel loved in every way. I tried hard to be a good role model, but I kept wondering what else I could do to make things better.

We managed to get through some difficult, dark days together, which made me even more determined to make it on my own. However, sometimes the financial struggles were more than I could bear. Some nights I would cry myself to sleep thinking about the daily phone calls from the creditors. I just couldn't seem to make ends meet. How would I be able to take care of all our needs?

Of course, I was too proud to ask for help. And I swore that when I finally got back on my feet, I would never serve my children macaroni and cheese again! I became a garage sale junkie, turning trash into treasures.

One day, 21-year-old Michael, who'd taken over as head of the household, came home from a college class and discovered that the security code to the garage door wasn't working. He went to a neighbor's house and called me. My first thought was, *They couldn't have shut off our electric.* I came right home and let myself in with my key. The house was quiet and still. No clocks ticking, no refrigerator humming...because there was no electricity! I immediately called the gas and electric company, and we worked out a payment plan. Our power was quickly restored, but my struggles were far from over.

As time went on, however, I began to feel a certain peace and contentment within. It was different being alone; I no longer had to walk on eggshells. When I was married, I held my breath everyday because I never knew what I was coming home to. Now, I no longer had to deal with fights or arguments. Unfortunately, my new sense of well-being didn't pay the bills.

I remember one Christmas when I truly could not afford to buy presents for my children. That Christmas Eve, a box mysteriously appeared on our front porch. Written on the box was *Merry Christmas to the children—from Santa!* To this day, I still don't know who the kind angels were that left those presents. I do know that their thoughtfulness made that Christmas a very happy time for us. Their kindness was the greatest gift I could have received.

Even though it was tough raising three children alone, it's because of that kind of generosity that I always felt compelled to help others whose needs were greater than mine. Not only was it rewarding to help someone else, it kept me busy and gave me less time to feel sorry for myself.

We may have been poor, but I felt rich because of the genuine friends with which we were blessed. I also felt so lucky to have three healthy children. They had their share of sports-related broken bones, chicken poxes and allergies, but for the most part I was spared constant trips to the doctor.

During our regular family meetings, my children and I would gather around the kitchen table to discuss chores and responsibilities, as well as their school events and sports schedules. Morgan tabbed these sessions our Windex Management Meetings.

Although Michael was now in college and Morgan wasn't far behind, they both still helped take care of Blake, especially since I had to focus on my training and consulting career. My work was very demanding at that time, but it opened doors for me and provided opportunities for success.

I eventually went on to become a national educator for an international company that produces educational materials for beauty schools. The job allowed me to travel and meet teachers from all over the country. It also made me take a serious interest in educating others within the industry, which led me to develop a series of seminars based on customer service and leadership. My intention was to help people reach their potential and take charge of their own success. At the same time, I became interested in taking my speaking skills to the next level, so I also became a professional motivational speaker.

Although I was busy, my life was beginning to settle a bit. And then one day out of the blue, I met the man of my dreams. He was charming, witty, kind and caring, traits that all worked for me. We immediately hit it off and began moving forward to start a new life together. It's amazing how the right person can change your life in all the right ways. I soon discovered that trusting someone empowers you to do things you could never have imagined.

Although the future can often seem predictable, sometimes it plays out in incredibly mysterious ways. I found myself wondering how it was possible that one very eligible man in his early fifties practically ended up on my doorstep. Was it simply by chance that this man who'd been born in Detroit ended up being my soul mate? It couldn't have been a coincidence that he moved in directly across the street from me. I believe that everything happens for a reason, and whatever *this* reason was, I couldn't have found a better partner with whom to share my life journey.

We had a beautiful 19th-century wedding at a quaint country village museum not far from where we lived. We were all together for the first time, our beloved family and our dearest friends. Our combined children and grandchildren, dressed in period attire, stood up for us as our attendants.

Everyone gathered in the colorful garden of wildflowers, anxiously awaiting the horse-drawn carriage to arrive. The air still held the dampness from an early morning shower, which prompted the village coordinator to suggest that we move the ceremony inside. I wouldn't hear of it.

"The rain *will* stop," I told her. "And we will be married in the gardens at high noon. A vintage baseball game will follow the ceremony, and we'll end the day with a fabulous pig roast served with an authentic 19th-century menu."

And the rain did stop. Shortly before noon, the horses approached just as planned, drawing a beautifully decorated carriage. Seated inside were Morgan; my second father, Red; and me.

With our full-length hoop skirts spilling over the side, and Red sitting proudly in his top hat and tails, it was just like a scene from the movie *Gone With the Wind*.

As the village fiddlers played their own version of *Here Comes the Bride*, Red was honored to give me away to the man he considered "the best thing that ever happened to me." As for me, I was thrilled to be marrying the man of my dreams.

Real love—it was merry and it was magical. I had to wonder if finding my soul mate meant that I had finally won a battle in my life? Maybe...but I was soon to discover that I certainly hadn't won the war.

It has now been six years since our nineteenth-century dream wedding. John is still the rock that keeps me grounded. I guess the third time really is a charm. He believes in me and helps me continue to believe in myself. Communication and respect are our keys to happiness. I communicate and he respects me! Imagine that.

When he proposed, he promised that he would make me laugh every single day. It didn't take long for me to discover that he wasn't kidding. The best part is, now he does it without even having to try!

John and I are known for finding humor in every situation and enjoying each day of our lives. We often travel to intimate destinations and also enjoy being on a golf course. And, like most grandparents, we love spending time with our six grandchildren. Each one of them adds a special element to our lives.

Life was finally picture perfect...until I was forced to face the greatest tragedy of my life.

It was then that my ability to trust was challenged like it never had been before. It was true that life had thrown me a few curveballs over the years, but somehow I continued to smile each time I stepped up to the plate. I managed to plow through years of tragedy, crisis and unavoidable disasters, all of which had been out of my control. But just when you think you've seen or heard it all, the unthinkable comes out of nowhere and turns your world upside down.

Nothing could have prepared me for what was about to happen or the emotional impact that it would have on our lives. But maybe if I had understood what to look for, I could have been more vigilant. Everyone should have the tools and the power to protect their family.

That is why I decided to write this book.

Chapter 5

It was a beautiful warm, sunny day, not much different than any other spring Sunday except that today was Mother's Day. What a joy to be among the millions of mothers who are able to celebrate such an occasion. The weather was certainly better than it had been all month, and the frequent rain we'd had meant the lawns were bright green and the flowers were beautiful.

Today, just like every holiday, Red and Shirley had invited us all over to their house. Shirley, who was like a mother to me and one of the most positive influences in my life, was always hosting some kind of party and enjoyed outdoor entertaining the best. And she had the perfect spot for it. The yard surrounding the in-ground pool, patio, two-tiered deck and gazebo looked like a park.

The tulips were in bloom and spread magnificent color patterns across the yard. I was admiring the umbrella tables that also added a splash of color when I heard the phone ring inside. I ran in the house and answered it on the second ring,

It was natural for me to answer Red and Shirley's phone since I spent a great deal of time with them. My hair salon was attached to their house, and I even had my own room so I could stay when the winter weather got nasty. My children loved that they could visit me at work and spend time with Grandpa Red and Grandma Shirley, who always welcomed the company.

Since I'd already spoken to Michael that morning and Blake was with me, I thought I knew whose voice I'd hear on the other end of the line.

"Happy Mother's Day, Mom!" Morgan exclaimed. "I miss you so much—I wish I could be there with you." Although I was happy to hear from my daughter, I heard something unusual in her voice.

"Thank you, sweetheart. Is everything okay?" I asked with some trepidation.

"I have something to tell you and today seems like the appropriate time to do it," she answered.

I knew this day would come. I had an idea of what she was going to tell me, but I was afraid to hear it. She lived so far away, and I dreaded the thought of being a long-distance grandmother. I handed the phone to Mama Shirley who was standing beside me in the kitchen. She was in the middle of cooking a fabulous roast pork dinner, with stuffing, mashed potatoes and all the trimmings.

The kitchen was beginning to fill up with guests, all who were now staring at me. Mama was still talking to Morgan, and I was pretty sure of what my daughter was telling her. I looked at my husband and whispered, *"She's pregnant!"*

My eyes welled up with tears and everything stood still. How bittersweet! She was still my little girl and yet so grown up. She was in her twenties but looked sixteen. I was her age when I had my first child but somehow I'd thought I was more mature and ready for motherhood.

When Mama shouted for joy, my suspicions were confirmed. My little girl was going to have a baby! Those words immediately took me back to Morgan's Polly Flinders dresses, all those beautiful prints with wide cross-stitch patterns across the top. I thought about the cute little patent leather shoes and her collection of porcelain dolls that had been put away for safekeeping. I had saved them all, hoping she would pass them on to her own daughter someday. As I stood in the warm kitchen, surrounded by family and friends, Morgan's life passed quickly before my eyes.

I remembered the day just before her kindergarten school play. I told her how pretty she looked even though she was missing the right side of her bangs. That morning she'd picked up a pair of her child safety scissors and decided to play hairstylist after watching Mommy in her beauty salon.

I remembered taking her to dance lessons every Tuesday after school, and to her dance recitals, where she got to show off her talent on the big stage. What an elegance that little girl possessed in her make-up and ballet slippers. She would pirouette so gracefully, then quickly swap her slippers for tap shoes and dance like a soldier to the tune of *Anchors Away*. We also enjoyed several years together in Girl Scouts and held many campfire outings in our backyard.

As my thoughts continued, I was oblivious to everything around me. My head was swimming with memories. I especially remembered the tea parties we used to have with real tea and cookies. Morgan would dress up in plastic heals and a feather boa, and we would sit around her little table with her dolls. I also remember the scorching days of summer when she and Michael would fill a fifty-gallon drum with cold water and jump in from the front porch to cool off.

Before I knew it, we had sleepovers with girls sprawled in sleeping bags across my living room floor. They spent hours fixing each other's hair and makeup. The house smelled like a beauty salon and my kitchen like a restaurant. I had such fun preparing snacks for them, and I used the girls as guinea pigs for all my new recipes. Needless to say, I never planned to get much sleep on those nights.

Back in Mama's kitchen, I stood staring out the window while everyone was wishing Morgan congratulations on the phone. I felt removed from this Mother's Day party. My brain went into flashback mode, to when she was just sixteen.

I saw Morgan in a lovely teal dress, standing next to Michael, who looked so handsome in his jet-black tuxedo. They anxiously awaited the arrival of the white stretch limo that was bringing her date—who also happened to be Michael's best friend— before picking up Michael's date. It wasn't hard to believe my kids were going to the prom together. They had always been close growing up and managed to remain very good friends all through high school. And like a good big brother, Michael was always watching his sister's back.

Equipped with my camera, I took shots from every angle to capture her lovely dress and every curl in her hair design. After losing so many pictures in the fire, I could never take enough photos of my children.

After the prom was over, Morgan and I spent the whole weekend talking about the wonderful time she had, what everyone wore and, of course, how the other girls had worn their hair.

Lastly, I had a vision of her packing her compact car full of clothes, shoes, memorabilia and Cabbage Patch dolls as she prepared to start her adult life in North Carolina.

When I finally got handed the phone, she gushed, "Mom, can you believe you are going to be a grandmother?"

Of course, she couldn't see my eyes fill with tears when I said, "Honey, I think it's wonderful. If you're happy, I'm happy. It's just so hard to believe...where has the time gone? You were just *my* little girl, and now you're going to be a mom!"

Ever since Morgan moved away, I'd visited her in North Carolina often. She and I had a very different relationship now. Not only was I enjoying getting to know her husband, Mitch, but I also was suddenly her new best friend.

Morgan wanted a perfect life for her new child. She also wanted a happy life for herself and occasionally asked me for advice. She didn't want to make the same mistakes I'd made in the past. We shared a lot of history during those visits.

One day while I was visiting and helping prepare the nursery, she sprawled across the bed, tucked a pillow under her arm and asked me a startling question. "Mom, if you had such an unhappy marriage, why did you have me?"

Without hesitation I said, "You sweet thing, a child is a gift from God. We never know how long we'll have them, or what circumstances they come with, so you love them unconditionally and enjoy them every single day. Having you was never a question. I truly believed you were coming into this world for a reason.

"The happiness Michael brought me seventeen months before was something I'd never imagined. I cradled him and held him close to my heart as often as I could. He brought me a sense of happiness I'd never known before. So when I was expecting you, I have to admit I did worry about sharing my love between the two of you, but when you were born it was truly effortless to love you both. Motherhood can be a tiring, frustrating, endless job. But it is one that comes with more rewards than any amount of money or recognition can bring. A positive attitude and belief in yourself will get you through anything. Always remember, if you love yourself first, you will be capable of loving others. We do not always make the best choices, or love for the right reasons, but a mother's love is unconditional."

After winding the musical mobile on the crib, I'd put my arms around her and told her again about the night she was born.

"It was a warm June night, and I had planned to go see Frankie Valli and the Four Seasons that evening. I was a little annoyed when my water broke that afternoon...I was already three weeks past my delivery date. I'd thought to myself—can't this wait one more day? Ironically, I found out the next morning that the concert had been cancelled for some unknown reason.

"As I lay in the hospital bed after you were born, tears streamed down my face. A nurse came in and asked why I was crying. I told her how happy I was to now have a little boy *and* a little girl. She looked at me with her head tilted and said, 'Young lady, those are not the tears of a happy new mother.'

"So I told her my plans to divorce your father. I confessed to her that I couldn't imagine raising two small children on my own, knowing I'd have to leave them to go back to work. Her voice was comforting as she told me that she understood. She knew the difficulty I had to face but told me that I was not alone. Somehow, I had the feeling that she had already walked in my shoes. She reminded me again of my strength and determination, and shared a few stories of her own. That night proved to me once again that laughter is the best medicine. I left the hospital with the confidence that raising my two babies with one loving parent was better than the present situation I was in."

It had been shortly after Morgan was born that I'd found the courage to end my abusive marriage. Even though we'd been married for seven years and had two small children together, I never looked back. Now, I kissed my grown daughter on the cheek and said, "You and Michael both deserved so much better. We all did."

It was wonderful to hear her say, "I love you, Mom. And I really appreciate everything you did to make our lives better. You had no car for a while, yet you managed to get us to the doctor, church and even the grocery store. How did you do it all, Mom?"

What doesn't kill us makes us stronger, I thought to myself.

I cupped my hands around her cheeks and told her, "It wasn't all that bad. We had a small but comfortable home. You and your brother kept each other company while I did my chores. Our door was always open to family and friends. I made sure to always have people around who lifted our spirits, and supported us with their love and understanding. As for me, I was very happy and content just spending time watching the two of you grow. We played games and listened to music. Your little laughs and giggles were enough to brighten my every day."

And, not surprisingly, they still are.

Chapter 6

On a brisk and sunny day, my plane touched down at a small but charming southern airport. After two or three go arounds, it was obvious that my luggage was not going to appear. I was speaking to the airline agent about my lost luggage when one of Morgan's friends ran through the doors, greeted me and said, "Hurry, there isn't much time!" I turned around and ran from the desk, then shouted back to the agent, "If you find my luggage, keep it. I'll call you later. My first grandchild is about to be born!"

We made it to the hospital just in time for the doctor to say, "Okay, Mom, get suited up. Your daughter is about to push for the last time." Up until that moment, I had no intention of being in the delivery room. But before I knew it, I stood in surgical scrubs next to a nervous Mitch as my precious grandbaby made her entrance into this wonderful, yet often cruel, world.

The emotions in that room were overwhelming. I squeezed Morgan and Mitch's hands while the nurses fussed with the baby. I could barely get the words out as I tried to tell them how proud I was of them.

The three of us just stood and watched in awe. We were counting fingers and toes, and admiring the crop of strawberry-colored hair on top of the tiny head that was now being covered with a little cotton hat. "Now *that* is a fashion statement," I said.

Morgan held her new baby girl, Chloe, on her chest, and then Mitch held her across his arm. I waited anxiously for my turn. A few minutes later, I cradled Chloe in my arms and introduced myself to her. At that moment, it seemed as though time stood still. I saw my own daughter as I remembered her from so many years ago, cradling her in the hospital on that lonely night when she was born. Now, it was hard to believe I'd come so far, that I was actually a grandmother. I always thought of grandmothers as being so much older. My perspective certainly had changed in a hurry.

As tears of joy ran down my face, I gently whispered to Chloe, "Hey diddle dumplin', my little pumpkin. I will always be here for you. I will protect you and always keep you safe, just as I did my own children. And that is a promise."

Her eyes were bright and followed mine as I spoke. She was so alert, it was as if she knew who I was and understood what I was saying to her. In her own way, she seemed to have responded to every word I said. For those few moments, it was just the two of us, developing our own special bond. I held her and fed her, patted her back and changed her tiny diaper. Because I couldn't stay long, Morgan and Mitch were very generous about sharing Chloe with me. Leaving would be much more difficult this time.

For some reason, it's human nature to want so much more for our grandchildren than we did for even our own children. I would never have believed, as I looked at this sweet, innocent new life, that in a few years she would become a devastating statistic.

As I helped Morgan get as comfortable as I could after her long and tiring delivery, I enjoyed watching her express the new joys of motherhood. While sitting in the chair across from her hospital bed, I recalled all the challenges of being a single mom. I thought about the issue of trust, about all the people who let me down and all the people who pushed me to be stronger. Despite all the hard times, I felt good about the person I'd become. I realized that fulfillment comes when you recognize the peace and contentment within you, when you understand that— nothing else matters.

I never could have imagined, after everything I'd already been through, that a situation could still arise that would make me feel so helpless and outraged.

And now I think about the words I said to my granddaughter on that joyful day of her birth, and how despite all my best intentions, I fell so very short of the promises that I made.

Chapter 7

Each visit with Chloe was filled with excitement. She always recognized me; her eyes would widen and her smile would grow big every time I'd arrive. I'd stay with her in the nursery, which doubled as the guest room, where I would cuddle with her and sing to her each night. In the mornings, she would peak her bright little eyes through the bumper pads inside her crib. I would play peek-a-boo right back. Then she would call, "Naaa-Naaa, Naaa-Naaa!" and point to the Noah's Ark animals on her bedding, as we laughed at each one. She loved crawling around on the plush carpet and pulling things out of my suitcase. She would play with my comb and brush for the longest time. Another little hair stylist in the making, perhaps?

A year later, my heart broke when Morgan called and told me that two-year-old Chloe had been left alone on the playground of her daycare center. It had been thirteen minutes before someone had discovered that she was missing.

Back when she was pregnant, Morgan, Mitch and I had interviewed this daycare center during one of my visits to North Carolina. It had seemed like a typical facility—

child-friendly, bright and colorful. It was a pleasant environment, with fully staffed classrooms that held wall after wall of creative artwork done by the children. When Morgan asked for my opinion of the place, I felt quite comfortable giving her my approval.

I told her, "As a parent, I'd have several requirements when picking a daycare center for my child. Most important to me is knowing that the child is safe. Next, I'd want to make sure the staff has integrity. And lastly, I'd want to be sure that the child is always under adult supervision." Since Morgan felt those criteria had been met, she was confident about enrolling Chloe at the center.

My only concern was the location of the building, which was on a main highway and surrounded by a chain link fence. The director of the daycare center assured us that the children were supervised at all times. They all went out together and came back in together, she said. So I wondered, how could Chloe have been left outside all alone for that long?

The staff had notified Morgan and Mitch immediately, asking them to pick up Chloe since she was understandably very upset. After apologizing for what had happened, the director explained, "The teacher was young and inexperienced, and we were very short staffed. I just fired her so you can be sure that won't happen again."

Despite the director's assurances, Morgan and Mitch were no longer comfortable leaving their baby girl in her care. They withdrew Chloe from that daycare center.

Next thing I knew, Morgan was pregnant again. With a new grandson on the way, I couldn't help but worry about my two grandchildren.

In the meantime, I continued to travel to North Carolina, each time eager to see how much Chloe had grown and what she had learned. When Christopher was born, Chloe immediately started acting like a little mother. She was very proud and very protective of her new baby brother.

It took me a year and a half to convince Morgan and Mitch to move back to New York for our grandchildren's sake. We wanted to be able to protect them and keep them safe. Not long after Christopher's birth, the kids and I were on a plane to New York, while their mom, dad, and Uncle Mike drove the moving truck up the East Coast.

It was wonderful having all of our family together for holidays, birthday parties and camping trips. One thing Chloe really enjoyed was sitting in my office, listening to me speak into a microphone as I rehearsed my motivational speeches. She was always fascinated by whatever Nana was doing. She and Christopher enjoyed standing on a chair at the kitchen counter, mixing cupcakes or blueberry muffins with me. No matter what we did, we always had a great time together.

It makes you wonder why it is that when things are going so incredibly well they can suddenly go so terribly wrong?

Chapter 8

I had always taught my two boys to never hit, punch or touch their sister—or any other girl—inappropriately. I have zero tolerance for any kind of violent behavior. They were to respect members of the opposite sex and never fall short of treating them as ladies. I taught them to build solid, healthy relationships with women, and above all else, to always establish a sense of trust. In addition, I taught Morgan to always look for the good in people and to put other's feelings before her own. I told her that if she treated people kindly and fairly, it would surely make a difference in her life someday.

During their adolescence, my children heard me repeatedly say things like, *Always communicate with respect*, or *You can achieve anything you want with a little effort and a lot of perseverance* or *Don't ever act like you're better than anyone else, but always believe that no one is better than you!*

I always lived by these mottoes and reminded my children of them often. Even Chloe had heard my words of wisdom and seemed to be living by them. So when I started noticing a change in her behavior, I became quite concerned.

The most obvious change was that she was starting to act very aggressive. She was louder than usual, and she no longer seemed to possess her meek and mild demeanor. I remember reprimanding her once for yelling at Morgan. I said, "Young lady! That is not an acceptable way to talk to your mother." I was shocked when she then stuck out her tongue and squinted her eyes at me. The more I thought about her behavior, the more perplexed I became. It seemed as though she was trying to tell us something. But what could it be?

Morgan wasn't happy with Chloe's new behavior, either, but she thought it was just a stage her daughter was going through. I suggested it might have something to do with her friends and activities at the new daycare center. When Chloe still hadn't improved after several months, I suggested that Morgan remove her from the program and put her in a different facility. I knew the decision had to come from her parents. Thank God they listened to me.

One afternoon while Chloe was still at that center, I planned a surprise lunch for the two of us. But when I went to pick her up, she began to cry and plead with me to let her stay with her friends. That was a major red flag because usually she'd jump at the chance to be with her Nana. Later, Morgan explained to

Mitch that I'd never interfere unless I felt something was really wrong.

Whenever I saw Chloe over the next few weeks, I realized that my otherwise sweet little girl was acting very irrationally. She was afraid to be left in a room alone, even if she was watching television. As soon as I would leave the room, she would follow me into the kitchen or bathroom, wherever I was going. Sometimes she would literally cling to me. However, when she went into the bathroom by herself, she would drag a chair or bench in front of the door. I thought that was really strange.

She had also been wetting the bed for several weeks, something she hadn't done in years. Her behavior became nasty at times, which was so out of character for her. One day, I finally took her in my arms and asked her to tell Nana what was bothering her. She put her little head down, and said, "Nothing, Nana."

During this time, Michael got married and Chloe was the flower girl in his wedding. On the night of the rehearsal, she seemed quite intimidated. I noticed her eyes moving rapidly as she walked down the aisle, as if she were scanning the pews for someone. I realized that she was afraid of all the unfamiliar faces in the church.

When the rehearsal was over, I took her aside and asked, "Do you remember the Barbie doll you told Nana about? The one with the hair that grows?" She nodded her head and said, "Yeeeeessss." I then told her, "If you walk down the aisle tomorrow and smile pretty while you're dropping your rose petals, I will give you Barbie to play with at the reception." I figured a little bribery from Nana is okay once in a while.

Right on cue, as she entered the country club reception, she stood before me with a big grin and said, "Nana, do you remember what you promised me? I did like you said and smiled all the way down the aisle." I took her over to the table, lifted the tablecloth, reached in my bag and handed her the Barbie doll. Although I thought she'd be thrilled to see it, she seemed less excited than I'd expected.

Although I knew something was eating away at her, I couldn't put my finger on what it was. Morgan and Mitch thought I was overreacting, but my gut told me otherwise. I'd been a mother for thirty years, and there's something to be said for a mother's intuition. It was so painful to watch all of this and not know what to do. I agonized over the situation and thought, What can I do for this precious child who thinks I'm her Fairy Godmother?

I had no idea the darkest days were yet to come.

Chapter 9

This brings us back to that fateful night, the one I will never forget. We all stood in the living room, just staring at the news broadcast on the TV. I felt like I was suffocating, that time was standing still. I couldn't move; it felt like someone had put weights in my shoes. My head was spinning like a top, and for a moment I thought I would pass out. This is definitely not happening to us, I thought. It can't be. I raised three children, and nothing like this ever happened before.

I swallowed hard as I tried to control my emotions. Slowly, I moved toward Chloe, reaching out and holding that little girl as tight as I could. Blinking back tears, I promised her with all my heart that no one would ever hurt her again. I then motioned for Mitch to call 911 immediately.

Words cannot describe how sick I felt. Morgan and Mitch grasped each other, unable to believe what they had just seen and heard. Moments later, they left the room, and I knew they were sobbing in each other's arms. As for me, I couldn't let go of my precious little granddaughter. I rocked her in my arms just as I had on the night she was born, less than five years ago. That was the same night I promised to protect her from any harm.

I couldn't imagine what she was thinking or feeling except for fear, which was written all over her face. I told her she did the right thing by telling us the truth. I tried not to overreact as I struggled to remain as calm as possible. Her parents returned to the room, and together we reassured her that in no way was any of this her fault. What had that man actually done to my innocent granddaughter? She was just a baby.

When the county sheriff arrived, he spoke to Morgan and Mitch outside, and then came back in and talked briefly to Chloe. The poor thing was totally shaken by what she had revealed just minutes before. Still, I couldn't believe how brave she was. After a brief conversation with my husband and me, the sheriff asked us to take Chloe out for ice cream so that he and her parents could file what would end up being a very lengthy report.

"And by the way," he said. "Please try and act as if nothing has happened."

I wanted to scream. *Act as if nothing has happened? Are you kidding me?* I'd just gotten the wind knocked out of me and could barely breathe. Someone had invaded my flesh and blood, violated what is most precious to me. And this guy is telling me to act as if nothing happened?

I was so angry! I was outraged! I suddenly possessed feelings I'd never had before. I truly feared what I might be capable of doing because I'd never felt such a horrible urge to viciously attack someone and make him pay for what he had done.

The three of us sat at a picnic table at what Chloe called "Ice Cream Island" and listened to every disgusting, despicable detail of what the bad man had done to her in a bathroom at Pepper Hill Daycare Center. It made John and I sick to listen to the words that fell from Chloe's mouth.

Although we were a wreck, she continued to calmly eat her chocolate cone covered with chocolate sprinkles. She almost seemed relieved to be telling us what had happened. She gave her Papa and me a wink, followed by a grin. I could barely control my anger, but I knew I had to stay in control for her sake. I covered my mouth with my hand because I thought I was going to be sick. It felt like I was on a roller coaster as all the blood rushed to my head. How could someone endanger the welfare of a child? Especially in a place where we thought she was safe. What should we do now? What is the next step in a situation like this?

How true it is that one split second can change a life forever. What could we have done to prevent this? I wondered. Where was the supervision? Why had we not recognized any of the signs that were right in front of us? Although my eyes filled with tears, my face stayed stoic as Chloe carried on a conversation with her Papa.

As she talked, I started connecting the dots that should *never* have to be connected.

Chapter 10

That was the first of many sleepless nights for all of us, including that precious and vulnerable little child.

When we took Chloe home earlier that evening, I asked the sheriff if the daycare center was accountable for what had taken place within its facility. He said all those questions would be answered in the coming days. He then asked if I would take Chloe, along with Morgan and Mitch, to The Bivona Center in the morning. I asked skeptically, "What's Bivona?"

I would find out later what a Godsend it is. At the time, I never knew such a place existed.

Later that evening, as the family gathered around my kitchen table, it was like you could cut the tension in the room with a knife. This was the place we'd always discussed things rationally, the place where we held our Windex Management Meetings. Now, you could feel the anger in the room. I didn't like what I was seeing or hearing from my children. They were as outraged as John and me. The adrenalin flowed, fists clenched, and then suddenly nobody was talking. Everyone was just staring at the ceiling or the kitchen walls. It was scary to see my grown children acting this way.

I felt like we had just returned from a funeral. I'd taught my children how to deal with disappointment, but I'd never seen them act like this. I said, "Come on, guys, we need to lighten up."

Blake, who was now nineteen, turned to me and said, "Mom, I have way too much respect for you to let you know what I'm thinking right now."

I said, "Honey, the law will take care of that man. Justice *will* be served. He will be stopped from ever committing this crime again. But right now, your sister and her family need our support, and we have to put our energy into helping our precious little girl get through this nightmare. Let's try to put our anger aside and focus on what Chloe needs right now."

With all the problems and difficulties that parents have to face, *this* is one issue they should never have to deal with.

The mood didn't change as we all tried to decide what needed to be done next.

Then, in a voice full of anger, Blake asked, "Mom, why would anyone do this to a *child*?"

I responded, "I don't have the answers, honey. If I did, this wouldn't be happening. In a perfect world, children wouldn't be at risk for something like this. But we don't live in a perfect world so it's time we find a way to do something about it."

Stress had played havoc on my body years before, and now I seemed to be reacting in a similar way. I was experiencing chest pains, shortness of breath and a crushing feeling that interfered with my sleep. I became extremely nervous and felt that I couldn't control what was happening to my body. So I had several heart exams, but they all proved negative. It was amazing, but the symptoms eventually started to disappear once I began working to help others.

Unfortunately, Morgan didn't have such an outlet for her stress, and it became a huge factor in her daily life. It took its toll on her just as it had on me years before. She developed serious health problems and ended up having the same surgical procedure that I did. Her husband was dealing with his own health issues as well, including anxiety and high blood pressure.

We all devoted as much time as we could to The Bivona Child Advocacy Center, a not-for-profit organization in Rochester that treats children who have been abused. The center offers a very child-friendly, relaxing environment so children do not feel threatened or intimidated in any way. Bivona's many partner agencies, counselors, investigators, and legal and medical professionals are all housed in one convenient location.

Bivona's mission is to reduce trauma, promote accountability, foster healing and advocate on behalf of child victims of sexual and physical abuse. The best part is they only interview the child once. What a blessing!

The support staff at this type of center works hard to meet the needs of not only the innocent victims but their families as well. It was the staff at Bivona that eventually helped me heal, transforming my negative thoughts and feelings into a more healthy perspective. They provided me with knowledge and understanding, and encouraged me to make something good come from this terrible situation.

Who would ever have thought I'd become an advocate for sexually abused children? Again, the staff at Bivona inspired me to channel my negative energy into something more positive. I began working to help make other families aware of this horrible crime. My goal was to empower people to be proactive so they would never have to know this kind of pain.

Bivona helped me grow as a person and made me realize that by volunteering I could make a difference in other people's lives. I joined their Speakers' Bureau and began doing my homework.

I came to realize that all children are potential victims. Sex offenders do not pick and choose. It does not matter who you are, where you live or what you own.

I also learned that when a child is sexually abused, it affects an entire community. Some people choose to ignore it and pretend that it never happened. Denial is a huge part of the cycle, especially if you know the victim personally. It's part of the human condition to want to avoid anything so horrible. However, people have no idea of the disastrous effects that denial can cause later in life.

Although many sexually abused children feel shame over what has happened, it's important that they understand it's never, ever their fault. Likewise, parents should not feel guilty or blame themselves for not protecting their children. No one is to blame except the abuser. Still, I often wonder who hurts more...the victims or the families who love them?

I was so grateful to all the professionals dedicated to helping abused children, including everyone at the district attorney's office. They communicated with us every step of the way, keeping us informed as to what was taking place as they prepared for trial.

In order to obtain an indictment against Michael Bennett, Chloe had to appear before a grand jury. The Bivona Child Advocacy Center and the D.A.'s team had explained the entire procedure to her beforehand. Due to their hard work, our brave little girl handled the grand jury with ease. Instead of reliving her terrifying experience and being intimidated all over again, she answered the questions smoothly, according to the assistant district attorney. Chloe's parents and grandparents were not allowed to sit in on the closed-court session to avoid any outside influence or non-verbal language as she was being questioned.

Needless to say, we were on pins and needles. When Chloe finally left the courtroom, she made a fist with her hand, held it under her chin and said to me, "Nana, just like you I got to talk into a microphone!" Even after everything she'd been through, she was still making me smile.

I'm not sure that people realize how much work goes into a prosecution. The assistant district attorney was extremely successful in handling our case. She got the job done; she got this child sex offender convicted and off the streets. One down, but how many more to go?

Chapter 11

It was Thursday, June 13, 2007. That morning, I drove downtown to the Hall of Justice with Morgan and Mitch. Needless to say, we were all a bit nervous. An uncomfortable silence settled between us as we parked the car in the ramp garage, headed upstairs through security and waited for the doors to open.

As everyone filed into the courtroom, I could feel the tension and anxiety around us. All eyes were on the man in the orange prison jumpsuit. For some reason, I thought time would make it easier to face Bennett, but when I saw him standing there I felt a shiver run through my body. Every inch of me turned stone cold. I immediately thought back to that horrible evening when I saw this same man in the same orange outfit on that 6:00 newscast that has caused me many sleepless nights.

It seemed as though we were waiting an eternity for this day to arrive, and now that it was here, I once again had a sick feeling in my stomach. Ever since that fateful night, we had seen Bennett all over the media, almost on a daily basis. We had also seen him at his arraignment following his arrest for abusing another little girl, and again at his hearing.

And when interest in his story seemed to wane, another child predator was soon gracing the evening news. It got to the point where it seemed that child sexual abuse was part of the daily broadcast. What is wrong with this picture? I wondered. This is out of control. I couldn't imagine how other families of victims were responding to all of this.

As I took my seat in the filled courtroom, I first glanced back at the news reporters and TV cameras that remained outside the door. Then I looked at Morgan and saw her eyes fill with tears. I could imagine the torture she must be going through. After all, this was *her* only daughter, too. As I looked at her, I realized I knew all too well how it felt to watch a child suffer. I took a deep breath, steeled my reserve and faced forward.

Although I tried to sit as still as possible, every muscle in my body strained to take action. I wanted to jump over the partition, grab that man in shackles and beat him senseless, causing him to feel the same pain that he'd brought to so many others. No, you must act like a lady and let the judge take care of him, I thought to myself. So instead of acting out my violent fantasy, I simply stared at him in utter disgust.

You worthless piece of crap. You deserve to go away and never come back. Never have the opportunity to touch another child. Never return to be a part of our community.

As these thoughts raced through my head, all those long months of healing seemed to disappear into thin air.

We listened for what seemed like forever to the arguments between the judge and the attorneys regarding the Pre-Sentence Investigation. Then the family of the other victim spoke first. When they were finished, I finally had my day in court.

*****

Following the objection of Bennett's attorney, I was allowed to address the court on behalf of Morgan and Mitch who were too distraught to speak. I stood before the crowded room, and spoke in a confident and controlled voice. I told Bennett exactly what we were feeling, the damage he had caused to my family and the disgrace he had brought to his.

I addressed the court. "Good Morning and thank you, Your Honor. I was told I couldn't speak directly to Mr. Bennett. Do you prefer that I speak to you or to him?"

The Court: "Whichever you feel more comfortable doing. Obviously he is not going to turn around."

I began, "My only hope is that over the next twenty-one years, Mr. Bennett, you wake up each morning thinking about the sleepless nights, the nightmares and the fear that you have instilled in these little girls, their parents, their grandparents and their entire families. It is also my hope that you think about the innocence that you robbed from these defenseless little girls, victims you paralyzed with fear and nearly frightened to death to keep your little secret, and the scars you have left them with for the rest of their lives.

My granddaughter Chloe will learn to cope through our support, but I assure you she will never forget what you did to her. Do you see the people in this room? These are people who wanted to have children and raise their families with pride and confidence, give them self-esteem and self-worth. Children are gifts from God. There are so many people in this world that would give anything to have a child. You, Mr. Bennett, took that privilege and truly abused it, and then used your own daughter to commit these despicable, horrific, unthinkable crimes. God knows how many times. You are truly not worth the trauma, the stress and the brokenness that you have caused these families. And yet somehow, you managed to win. You have violated my flesh and blood. You have devastated those most precious to me. Although forgiveness is very difficult at this time, today we will all begin the healing process.

I will never forget the look on my granddaughter's face when she told me about the bad man and what you did to her. It sickened me then as it stills does today.

None of the things that happened in our lives could have prepared us for that day. Thank God the Bivona Center was there to help us through that. We now have some closure, and we can finally move forward and spread awareness to other families. Hopefully our efforts will prevent others from experiencing the kind of emotional impact you left us with."

I stopped for a brief moment, expecting him to turn around and face me. I asked just one question of him. "Mr. Bennett, what happened in your life that was so bad that you had to violate ours?" There was an eerie silence, and no reply.

"Thank you, Your Honor," I finished.

I took my seat and felt like a washcloth hung out to dry, lifeless and drained of all feeling.

Then Bennett's ex-wife got up to speak. "Michael Bennett is a cold-hearted sociopath, a vicious monster who shows no remorse for his crimes. What father would use his own child to gain access to other children for personal sexual gratification? He deserves the worst possible incarceration to remind him daily of the pain and suffering we'll all endure as we try to repair our lives and help our children recover. He deserves the maximum punishment and consequence the judicial system will allow so that he pays for his crime, and our children can feel safe and secure again."

My heart went out to her and her family, especially her daughter. "Please, God," I prayed. "Help this innocent child have a normal life. Please give her the strength she needs to survive, and see that she is counseled so she may someday be able to accept real love."

I never made eye contact with Bennett, but I could feel the sarcasm in his voice as he stated his guilty plea in order to spare his victims from standing trial. He said he expected no forgiveness.

Good, because you'll get none from me.

He continued, "This has weighed heavily on my mind, and continues to weigh heavily on my mind to this day."

Oh, enlighten me! How can you act like you didn't know the damage you'd do? What could you possibly have been thinking when you were alone with your victims?

He then apologized to the victims' families, his own family and his ex-wife for the pain and trauma he caused them. He said that he spends every day in jail hoping and praying that everyone involved is getting better and will not continue to be traumatized by his actions.

Didn't you learn anything from your past mistakes?

He also said that he prays his actions will not have a long-lasting effect on the children.

Chloe trusted you, the parent of a little girl who just happened to be her best friend.

Bennett told the judge that he's a caring person, and he hopes his time in prison will afford him the opportunity to get the help he needs.

The Court: "Mr. Bennett, I have read over the Pre-Sentence Investigation. It's one of the thickest I have ever seen and much of it is letters from people whose lives you have touched by your evil actions, and I am not going to redact any of the letters from here. They are all going to go with you to prison.

"I want to thank the people who spoke here today. It takes courage to get up and speak in front of a large group, especially after what you all have been through.

"The two people who aren't here are the ones I feel the most sorry for. I couldn't imagine going through this trial and having these two little girls having to sit on this witness stand and look at you, the crowd and audience of the press, and have to talk about something that happened to them. I think the devastating affect of that would have been almost as bad as what you did to them. It would have been all over the papers and for years they would have to read about their case, and I don't know if their parents and families could have protected them. All the counseling in the world probably wouldn't help them then.

"If this were your daughter, what would you want someone sitting up here to do to the person that did that to your child?"

Bennett answered, "The same exact thing that is happening to me, Your Honor."

The Court: "Times one hundred, I assume you'd say."

Bennett answered, "Absolutely."

The judge was ready to read the verdict.

We sat holding hands, Morgan, Mitch and me. We already knew what the verdict would be, but hearing it read inside the courtroom brought us a small measure of comfort. We breathed a collective sigh of relief, knowing that this sick pervert's twisted life as a child abuser now had been brought to a screeching halt.

The Court: "When twenty-one years came up, I really had to think about it, but I put the interest of the two children before what I really thought the sentence should be. To me, forty-six years is not even enough. Your history is awful.

"We argued about the facts of the 1991 burglary, whether you broke into that house, abducted the woman and took her back to your apartment. Whatever the facts and circumstances are, it appeared to be random, probably sexual in nature. You got five years probation. You were not registered as a sex offender then.

"In 2004, we had the EWOC and aggravated harassment. Once again, calling at random, getting a ten-year-old boy to masturbate. You pled guilty, got sixty days in jail and three years probation.

"I think that was the first time you called it random. Absolutely not. Some of the letters in here said that this was a repeated behavior, and there's no doubt in my mind that that's the only time you got caught.

"You are a walking time bomb. Through probation, they put you in sex offender counseling, to see what we could do to try to stop you from victimizing anyone else.

"You've been going to your counseling sessions, and your letter from your attorney says you missed a few because of work. The day you abused one of the girls, you go right to counseling just like nothing happened. Obviously counseling was a waste of time.

"You would think that all the bells and whistles would be going off from your first two convictions that you're a danger to everybody, but nobody knows until it is too late, until you victimize two more people."

As the judge continued, he read the diagnosis from the defendant's therapist, who described him as someone with Pedophilia and Antisocial Personality Disorder, and who said he wouldn't benefit from sex offender treatment.

The judge continued. "That, in sum and substance, means you're not sick. You don't have an illness, what you have is a compulsion. This compulsion is never going to go away. That's why the legislature is working so hard to get through this new statute about potential civil commitments for people that are going to pose a danger when it is time to be released.

"When released, Parole is going to look at this Pre-Sentence Investigation. You're going to go through a SORA, which is the Sexual Offender Registration. You're going to have another evaluation when you're done, probably evaluation after evaluation, and there is the potential that in 21 years or 17 years—which is when parole will probably let you out, which I don't have any say about it— this new statute will kick in, probably over the next 17 years or so. They'll probably fine-tune the civil commitment because it's a new statute, but if you still pose a danger, hopefully that civil commitment will keep you away from all the other children, all the other potential victims besides children, for as long as humanly possible."

I don't believe child molesters can change, but you can bet your life their victims' lives will be changed forever.

The Judge looked directly at Bennett and said, "You said you were scared of going to prison. You should be scared. It's not going to be easy for you, but it is still minor in comparison to the way you made those girls feel. You're going to have a long period of time to think about your actions. I'm not really concerned about you being sentenced for rehabilitation. This is punishment."

The devastation you have brought to your own family, as well as to others, is unforgivable. You are the scum of the earth.

The judges final words to Bennett were, "The true finality for these families and the girls comes from your having waived your right to appeal. This is closure."

I felt an enormous amount of respect for the assistant district attorney when she stood up and said she couldn't risk the lives of these five year olds. She also stated that this sentence will protect our community for a significant amount of time, and when the defendant is released from prison, these girls will already be adults.

She finished by saying, "Judge, I have to say I am so unbelievably impressed with the families involved in this case. For once, I have seen three families do the right thing from the get-go. They have all supported their children by getting them counseling and putting their interests first. I thank each one of the families who are here in court today on behalf of their children for doing the right thing. These are fantastic people who did not deserve any of this."

Later in a television interview, she said that the resolution of the case, which included Bennett's agreement to waive his right to an appeal, was in the best interest of the children involved. She also told the press what she had stated in court, that she agreed with the families that 21 years was not enough. She said, "I was never going to roll the dice with these children's lives, in getting justice and protecting them. I have seen first hand that juries don't always believe our children and often feel their testimony isn't enough."

As we left the courtroom, we declined any interviews with the media. I did, however, agree to an off-camera interview with one of the local television stations at a later date. I felt that if I didn't come forward and comment on the proceedings, I would be doing a disservice to the community. I was torn because my sole concern was to protect Morgan and her family, while at the same time, I thought the more people I could reach with my message the better. Regardless, I had to be careful that I didn't say anything that would compromise the ongoing investigation of the daycare center.

When I finally spoke to the press, I said, "It's unthinkable what happened!"

I continued, "When this story broke, it was reported like any other news story. But what about the ramifications of what happened, the lives that were broken?

Then the reporter asked my feelings about the daycare center.

I replied, "What kind of daycare staff doesn't know what is going on in its own facility? How can it not inform parents of such a serious criminal act? Why did we have to see this man on TV after he committed yet another crime before we found out what he did to my granddaughter?"

I still wondered if Chloe would have ever come forward and told us what happened if she hadn't seen Bennett on the news. What if he had never been caught? How long might she have kept this to herself and lived in fear of his threats? I shuddered to think of how much worse this could have been.

The news reports all said the same thing..."This is an isolated incident." Every time I heard those words I wanted to scream. We need to be smarter and more informed. Every community needs to take back control and put an end to such abuse.

In a conversation I had after the trial with District Attorney Michael Green, I asked him how many cases of child sexual abuse are reported each year in Monroe County.

He told me many cases are reported to investigative agencies. Of those referred, six to seven hundred cases a year actually make it to the District Attorney's Office. So many other stories go untold.

Green also said that initial reactions are critical. "If parents keep an open mind and don't immediately show disbelief, then the outcome will be much more positive for the child. Many people immediately feel that what happened will cause the family embarrassment. They focus too much on the shame."

He went on to say that in many cases people have unrealistic expectations. If there is a time lapse between the actual incident and when it's reported, it becomes much more difficult to obtain DNA proof. He also told me of the enormous efforts of the assistant D.A.'s office to convict these sex offenders on an ongoing basis.

Over a cup of coffee one morning, my friend Jean and I were trying to make sense of it all. I was writing a speech on the topic when I looked up at her and said, "Why do you think all this happened?"

After all, I always believed things happen for a reason. But what possible reason could there have been for this?

She put down her cup and said, "God took something *evil* and used it for good." She then paraphrased a verse from the Bible that made some sense of the situation.

I thought about what she'd said for a moment, then asked for the first time, "But why *her?*"

Jean replied, "Because of what you're doing this very moment, looking for ways to promote awareness to other families, to prevent other children from becoming victims. Your efforts to save one child or one family from this horror will make something good come out of what you've been through." Then she added, "You have a passion for helping people, and it shows in everything you do and say. People need to here you speak."

I thanked Jean for sharing her thoughts with me. I gave her a hug and said, "Then I guess I'd better get to work."

Sharon Grace

Chapter 12

After spending a great deal of time at both The Bivona Child Advocacy Center and The National Center for Missing and Exploited Children, I got involved with both organizations. I volunteered, helped with several fundraisers and joined their Speakers' Bureaus. I discovered the endless opportunities that exist for those who want to get involved. With my encouragement, many of my family and friends did just that.

Although it helped to be doing something proactive, we all continued on an emotional roller coaster for quite some time. I know that life is about constant change and our attitudes determine many of our reactions. Regardless, it wasn't easy to just put what had happened behind us and move on.

Morgan and Mitch are still trying to come to terms with the horrific event that dramatically altered their lives. They maintain an open line of communication with Chloe and Christopher. They keep their eyes open for unusual behavior. They have learned that if children are acting out, then they may be reaching out.

As for Chloe, she is still struggling with the ever-present fear. Thankfully, she has benefited greatly from counseling. In some way, every member of our family is still impacted by what happened to us two years ago. And we're just one family out of thousands that suffer from the effects of child sexual abuse every year.

Right after we'd learned what had happened to Chloe, we created a code word for her to use when she wanted to talk about her ordeal. Thankfully, she knows that Nana and Papa will always listen to her.

One day after a session at Bivona, Chloe and I were having lunch at my kitchen table when she looked at me very seriously and said, "Nana, were you a human before you got old?"

I said, "Excuse me?"

She said again, "Were you a human before you got old?"

"Do you think I'm old?" I asked.

"Well...YEAH," she said. "How old are you?"

I immediately said, "About twenty-nine."

She said, "Huh, you're the same age as my mom."

I grinned and said, "You silly girl." She got off her chair and put her arms around me.

"Nana, I just wanted to make you laugh," she explained.

The she added, "Nana...today is a new day!"

Her positive attitude was obviously a direct result of her counseling session.

We have also learned to expect the unexpected. For instance, one day I was shopping at the mall for Chloe's birthday party with Morgan and the kids. Chloe wanted something that Morgan had already told her she couldn't have. So of course, my smart little granddaughter decided to ask her Nana.

I said, "Honey, what is so important that you have to have it?"

"I want that red balloon on a string," she replied.

I said, "You already have plenty of red balloons at home for your party."

"NO, I want *that* red balloon!" she yelled.

Another power struggle, I thought

When I told her she couldn't have it, she began to cry and throw a temper tantrum, which was totally out of character. I was really shocked at her behavior.

As she continued to cry hysterically, I took Christopher from the store and went to my car.

When Morgan brought Chloe to the car, she continued the inappropriate behavior. She unbuckled her seatbelt, jumped out of the car and ran across the parking lot still crying and carrying on.

You can imagine the scene!

Morgan chased her down and got her back in the car. All the way home, though, I watched her hands flying and feet kicking through the rearview mirror. She continued to cry and scream at both of us. When I gave her a bottle of water that she'd asked for, she threw it at Morgan.

As I pulled into my driveway, I noticed several police cars pulling in behind me. They were holding cell phones, talking to the County Sheriff's Office and Child Protective Services as they paraded up my driveway. After a lengthy conversation with me about what had happened at the mall, they compared stories with Morgan and a very frightened Chloe. Short of inviting them in for dinner and offering them my first born, it was not easy to convince them we did not "abduct" this child or "abuse" her in any way. At first, I was really annoyed and angry at their questioning. Then I realized—the system is working! Somebody called to report something that did not look right!

We finally told them who this little girl was and why she was having behavioral issues. I also told them I was invited to be the guest speaker for The Bivona Child Advocacy Center fundraiser that was a few weeks away. I thought, *Do I look like a criminal?* But that's exactly the point. Most sex offenders look fairly normal. I finally ended up thanking them for following up on what could have been a devastating crime.

Some people have asked me, "What is considered child sexual abuse?" After months of research, I have discovered that most definitions are in agreement. Basically, it's defined as any sexual activity or exposure between an adult and a minor child. It also includes any forced sexual action, such as touching or fondling, oral sex, intercourse or pornography.

As an advocate, I am constantly telling people that if they suspect child sexual abuse, they should report it immediately to the police. If it looks wrong or feels wrong, it probably is. Trust your gut, act on instinct and err on the side of caution. We must never assume our children are safe!

Child sexual abuse can lead to many social, emotional and physical problems if not dealt with at an early stage.

Sometimes children are afraid to come forward with the truth. They fear they'll get in trouble or not be believed. They don't want anyone to think that what happened is somehow their fault. I always found it easy to talk to people, having learned how to express myself at an early age. However, it is not as easy for others, especially young children.

We need to be more aggressive in resolving this issue. Most of us have the common goal of keeping our children safe. No one wants a sex offender living right next door to them or having access to the areas where their children play.

So what do we do about it? For starters, we can empower our children with safety skills. Talk to them about inappropriate touching, threats, secrets, even online abuse and computer safety.

It is our job as parents, grandparents, childcare providers and teachers—and anyone who is directly involved with children—to communicate, educate, and listen to our young people.

Through all of my life experiences, listening has always enabled me to make a real difference.

According to The National Center for Missing and Exploited Children:
- Teaching children the "stranger danger" message is no longer effective.
- Statistics show that children are more likely to be victimized by someone they know, love or trust. This is true for both abductions and sexual abuse.
- One out of every four girls, and one out of every nine boys, will be sexually abused by the time they turn eighteen.

According to The Bivona Child Advocacy Center:

- Ninety percent of victims know their offender. Again, it's usually a family member, friend or adult with authority.
- Everyday in our own community, children are beaten, abused and neglected by the adults they trust.
- Every six minutes, a child is sexually abused in the United States.

My purpose now is to raise and increase family awareness and offer hope to those who have been impacted by child sexual abuse.

*****

For weeks following the verdict, I continued to wrestle with the anger and other emotions I'd felt for the last year and a half.

Once a friend asked me, "Have you forgiven him?"

I thought about it for a minute and finally said, "No!" I took a deep breath and continued, "Forgiveness is a process, one that takes a very long time. Simple things in life are easy to forgive. The complicated things that hurt people, cause unbearable pain, create mistrust and leave permanent scars are not as easily forgiven."

I do know, though, that forgiveness has always been the only thing that's allowed me to move forward and heal.

For instance, my father and I had a strained relationship for many, many years, but before he passed away, his last wish was to bring our family back together. I spent more time with him during his last four days than I had in the previous twenty years. But out of all those years of negativity came something positive—my family was reunited again. Just months after my father's death, we celebrated our first holiday as a family in many years...and actually had a good time. My mother and I were able to pick up the pieces and enjoy each other's company, sometimes even laughing about the good old days.

This is what I have learned:

People have to be accepted for who they are, not who we want them to be.

You can't hold a grudge forever because the weight will just drag you down.

Placing blame doesn't resolve the past, it only makes it eat away at you.

Forgiveness is more for me than for the other person.

An open heart invites kindness and is more accepting of love.

This kind of thinking has allowed me a new freedom, a new happiness.

When the trust is broken, like a pencil snapping in half, it's never the same again. Trust, once broken, takes a tremendous amount of strength and effort to rebuild. Sometimes it takes days, months, even years to forgive.

I am not completely there yet. But I am working on it.

*If you are a victim or someone you know is a victim of sexual abuse, immediately call 911 or your local Law Enforcement.

Resource Guide:

Local:
Bivona Child Advocacy Center
Rochester, New York 14608
Telephone: 585-935-7800
Website: www.bivonacac.org

National Center for Missing and Exploited Children, NY Branch
275 Lake Avenue
Rochester, New York14608
Telephone: 585-242-0900
Facsimile: 585-242-0717
Website: www.missingkids.com
Toll-free Hotline: 1-800-THE-LOST (1800-843-5678)

Nationally:
National Center for Missing & Exploited Children
Charles B. Wang International Children's Building
699 Prince Street
Alexandria, Virginia 22314-3175
Toll-free Hotline: 1-800-THE-LOST (1-800-843-5678)
Fax: 703-274-2200

Worldwide:
The CyberTipline
TTY line: 1-800-8267653
Website: www.cybertipline.com

Sharon Grace